WHY ARCHITECTS MUST *Write* a BOOK

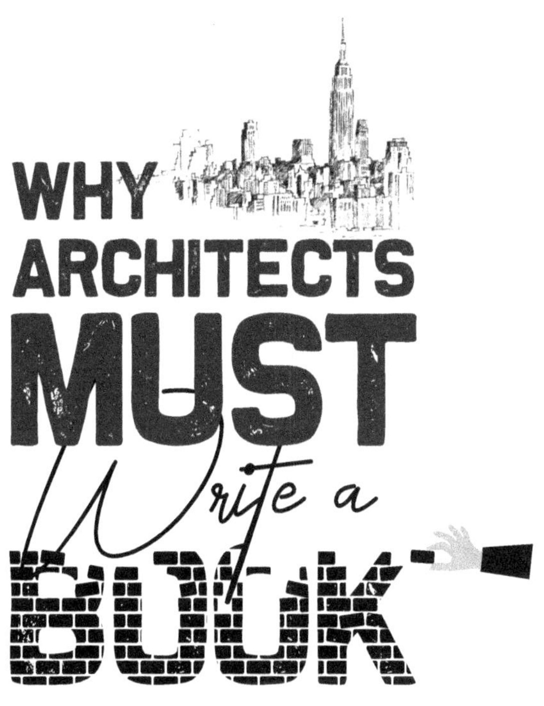

DINESH VERMA

WITH ANKUR HORA

Worldwide Published by
Pendown Press

PENDOWN PRESS
An ISO 9001 & ISO 14001 Certified Co.,
Regd. Office: 2525/193, 1st Floor, Onkar Nagar-A,
Tri Nagar, Delhi-110035
Ph.: 09350849407, 09312235086
E-mail: info@pendownpress.com
Branch Office: 1A/2A, 20, Hari Sadan, Ansari Road,
Daryaganj, New Delhi-110002
Ph.: 011-45794768
Website: PendownPress.com

First Edition: 2021
Price: ₹199/-
ISBN: 978-93-5554-149-9

Layout and Cover Designed by Pendown Graphics Team
Printed and Bound in India by Thomson Press India Ltd.

CONTENTS

INTRODUCTION

Thank you for choosing this Book. **This Book could be the pivot point that inspires you to make your message kingsize and build your Business exponentially.** To make an enormous impact on the world and establish synergy with your clients, the way you have always craved. Architects have always been an integral part of building society and the world at large, that too very literally.

Architects have professional knowledge that can add value to people's lives when designing homes, offices, and other commercial establishments. Besides, **they also have valuable life lessons** to impart. They are masters at understanding the importance of a foundation well laid, a deadline met, optimum use of resources, and the value of planning before jumping to action.

They also have significant out-of-the-box brilliant innovations to contribute to the world. **These eco-friendly and cost-friendly innovations are essential to creating a sustainable ecosystem in the face of horrifying climate change repercussions.**

Architects can also help clients save one-time and running costs by sharing their in-depth knowledge, **thereby making their buildings Money Making Investments** instead of Cost-Intensive nightmares to run.

As an Architect, you have worked tirelessly and helped several people and institutions bring to life the office, home, or public space of their dreams. **It is time now to extend your reach and broaden your horizons.** Countless clients are waiting for the solutions that only you can provide and the expertise only you can render. They are waiting to find the Architect that is the perfect fit for their needs and aspirations.

Now you must be wondering how you can magically and magnetically reach out to your potential clients???

Writing a book is what will help you reach those people. A book written by you will instantly allow all your potential clients, your peers, and your community to identify you as the established Authority in your field.

Writing a book is an instant passport to credibility. It establishes your credentials as nothing else can.

Your Book is your calling card, your resume, your referrals, and your portfolio all rolled into one.

You can not afford not to write one!

You owe it to yourself, society and humanity to write one!

In this Book, Ankur Hora, my co-author, and I will give you concrete evidence of "Why Architects Should Write A Book."

We will also share a clear blueprint for writing the Book of your dreams and hold your audience captivated in a record time of 7 days by sharing the Magic Template with you.

The Magic Template

As you are determined to move out of your comfort zone and have chosen to take action to shift your life into top gear by choosing this Book, you deserve to be applauded for this courage. Therefore it is time to share with you this premium template.

This template will help you crystallise your thoughts, identify your potential clients, and establish your Authority in the industry. It will help you craft a Book that adds exceptional value to the reader's life and not just another book that will fail to transform your life or Business in any way.

Publishing a book is the first potent weapon in the arsenal of MM Methodology (Marketing Magnetism Methodology) referred to in the 2nd chapter.

We will teach you to become an Insta Book Influencer Which is the need of today's times and is a Proprietary Tool designed by me to have you write a book and *impact the world and your business and customer acquisition hugely and speedily.*

This powerful form of book writing has already helped various business owners and consultants from a wide range of industries.

Mr. Akshat Bansal's Insta Book Influencing has helped him sell Door Handles worth even 20 lakhs effortlessly.

Mr. A.C Sud has taken his Multi-Level-Marketing business to great heights through his Insta Book.

Mr. Raktim Singh has established himself as a thought leader in the world of Digitalization after his Insta Book came out.

Architect Rohit Surendra Nagia has had a major impact on his business with his 2 Insta Influence Books. He says he coverts 1 client every fortnight with ease now.

It's your turn now!

We know you can't wait to begin on your Book, so let's turn the page and move forward…

Who are we, and why should you listen to us?

My name is Dinesh Verma; I am an award-winning publisher, best-selling Author, popular speaker, and successful coach.

By the grace of the almighty, I have helmed the Gullybaba Publishing House Pvt. Ltd. for the last two decades and worked to make it the largest and No.1 Company in IGNOU Self-Help Books in the World.

Not willing to rest on my laurels, I worked to broaden my horizons and, thus the Pendown Press was conceptualized.

Pendown Press is an exclusive global platform for Entrepreneurs, Coaches, Speakers, Consultants, Academicians, Trainers, etc., who have something to share with the world, and believe in the impact of books on the Business and millions of lives.

We help you build a concept, write, publish and market your Book to influence the world with supercharged marketing. In the last few years, we have redefined publishing, thereby enabling writers to embark on their Star-studded journey to becoming an influential authority by writing and publishing a bestseller book in no time, creating more Income and Impact.

Till today, we have published 2200+ books in total, which cover fiction & non-fiction topics. I have worked with senior scientists, authors in India, UK, Dubai, and Ukraine. Many of our Authors have been selected by GOI for Beijing, South Africa, London, UAE, and other International Fairs in their official catalog for the respective countries.

I have also been blessed enough to have had an opportunity to meet the then President of India, Honourable Shri Pranab Mukherjee in the Rashtrapati Bhawan in the year 2014 and during our conversation I was inspired by him to write about the environment.

This got me thinking about writing about the environment in a manner that would be an interesting topic for the common person too. Then I used my knowledge of astrology and combined it with plantation that is much needed for the planet. So I shared how one can plant trees in a manner to ward off the negative effects of planets by planting the right trees through my book ***"Vriksh Lagaye Graho Ko Apne Anookool Banaye"***.

Then I was fortunate to have gifted this Book to the then respected Enviromen Minister, Dr. Harshvardhan at his Residence on Tees January Marg.

If anyone should know about the life-changing power of writing a Book, I should because all that I have achieved today began with writing a Book.

Having supported hundreds of Entrepreneurs, Coaches, Professors, Trainers, etc. become Published Authors, I am delighted to have a chance to grow book publishing with the mission to create 10,000 authors, thereby impacting 10 Million lives on this planet by circa 2025.

My Co-author Ankur Hora is a force to be reckoned with, a young, dynamic entrepreneur and innovator par excellence. **He is the founder and CEO of 'ecoste.' He was one of the pioneers who visualised the potential of WPC products in the country and went on to make 'ecoste' one of India's most popular brands in its industry.**

'Ecoste's' initiatives for the WPC industry are considered remarkable. They have been lauded and saluted by their peers and industry bodies for their untiring efforts, time spent, and expenditures made for creating micro-level awareness of the overall concept of WPC in the country. **Under Ankur's able leadership, they took up community outreach and focused on Architects, Builders, Interior Designers, Contractors, and Carpenters to educate and promote this innovative product as the first line.**

They developed extensive educative videos explaining WPC products and their applications. Their blogs, videos, promotional campaigns, educative seminars, and various other efforts have helped the entire industry understand and foray into WPC products.

Ankur's initiatives helped create an entire industry and had a massive impact on the economy by reducing imports and relieving the nation of the consequent Forex drain. Thanks to his pioneering efforts today, there are 100+ players in the industry, yet **'ecoste' is ranked as the industry's top players.**

Ankur is a master at driving sales, creating a buzz, and reaching out to potential clients. If anyone knows how to promote your product/message to reach your audience successfully and speedily, it is him.

CHAPTER 1

LAYING THE FOUNDATION TO SUCCESS: IT MATTERS THE MOST!

Often in my interaction with friends who are building their dream homes or offices, I have seen many of them feeling that they are not on the same page as their Architects. On the other hand, in his innumerable interactions with Architects, Ankur has consistently observed that they feel that their clients sometimes don't understand the pressure and constraints they operate under and expect them to meet unrealistic design and delivery standards.

Another time when I had the opportunity to speak at a gathering of Architects, I found that while they struggle with the same pain points and challenges as other entrepreneurs and business owners, there are specific challenges that are typical to their industry. During the panel discussion, I said there is a single solution to all your generalized and specific concerns; LAUNCH A BOOK!

For a few seconds, there was a stunned silence! Everyone looked at me like I had dropped a Bomb, and indeed I had.

A TRUTH-BOMB; that is what I had unleashed. Having coached and supported hundreds of entrepreneurs and business owners to become Published Best Selling Authors. I can say with complete Authority that the only thing standing between you and legitimate Super-Star Success in your field is a Best Seller written by you.

One day while Ankur and I were engrossed in an animated conversation over coffee, I brought up my experience of speaking on the panel with Architects. Having worked closely with Architects for long, he agreed with me 100 % that the answer to all their woes is indeed a Book.

That very instant, Ankur and I decided to pool in our knowledge and experience of driving success through tried and tested Road Maps created by us to write this Book that aims to guide Architects to write, publish and market their Book. Writing a Book guarantees their shift from chasing clients to being serenaded and sought after by clients.

Let's address the generalized pain points first;

- Struggling to establish yourself as an Authority in your industry?

- Struggling to build an edge over your competitors?

- Struggling to have a lasting impact on your clients.

- Struggling to generate leads or potential clients?

- Client meetings degenerating into negotiation battles at the level of flea market bargaining.

- Big potential clients playing hide-and-seek when it comes to setting up appointments.

- Tired of visiting networking seminars/organizations; where results are not proportional to the time and resources invested.

- Struggling to be perceived as an expert and to be taken seriously.

- Struggling to hire and retain talent.

- Competitors who are low on knowledge and expertise, providing inferior services, but quoting higher prices.

Sounds familiar???? Well, yes, of course! For these are your struggles. You have been battling with them for a long time with limited success. That, however, stops now because Ankur and I are here to empower you to overcome these challenges and limitations by writing your Book.

No! Don't worry; we have not forgotten about the pain points and challenges typical to your industry. Let's address them as well;

- The mismatch between you and your clients because they do not communicate their expectations clearly and precisely.

- Unrealistic design and delivery expectations from the client.

- Sticking to project deadlines in the face of challenges like licenses, sanctions, bureaucracy, and other factors totally beyond your control.

- Struggling to build trust with your clients in the face of multiple decision-makers, delayed reverts on samples, and other crucial decisions.

- Delayed payments affecting completion deadlines.

- The pressure and stress of coordinating and interfacing with multiple agencies and vendors simultaneously.

Yes! These too can be overcome and solved by writing a Book. Unbelievable, you say, well, that is what we are doing through this Book; making the impossible a reality.

Turn the page and let the magic unfold…

CHAPTER 2

THE BOOK: YOUR CALLING CARD, CV, LORs AND PORTFOLIO: ALL-IN-ONE

Ankur and I have been telling you that writing a Book is the solution to all your challenges. Now let's clearly and categorically tell you the 'How" and "Why."

As per the popular and effective 'MMM: Marketing Magnetism Methodology' to convert prospects into clients, it is essential to give them some "Leave- behind- Material" so that they can recall and remember you for a longer period and have your name imprinted on their subconscious mind.

What could be a better "Leave-behind-material" than a Book written by you?

Need Proof???

Here is irrefutable proof:

First, let's talk about the reasons that will generally benefit you when you write a book. Then we will list the specific reasons you as an Architect will overcome the challenges specific to your industry and contribute to the world.

Top 10 Reasons why you must write a Book!

1. The prefix 'Author' before your name lends Respectability and Authority to your name.

2. Being an Author creates a better perception of your profile instantly.

3. Generate a Passive Income; as you work once but keep getting paid forever.

4. Create a Dream Business.

5. Become a Role-Model and Inspire others to live better lives.

6. Generate thousands of Leads for your Business by becoming an Amazon Bestselling Author.

7. Free yourself from being Underpaid, Underestimated, and Undervalued.

8. Become Empowered to Charge your Worth.

9. Stand apart from the crowd and be perceived as an Expert in your field.

10. Expand your Personal and Professional Network by creating a good story, talking about a passion project.

Once you've authored a Book, you will notice a paradigm shift in your world:

1. Doors that were previously closed will be held wide open for you.

2. Those elusive, big clients who wouldn't give you the time of day will readily give you appointments. Your Book will work as your magnetic Calling Card.

3. Negotiations will become smoother, and people will not compare what you charge to others. Your Book will establish your worth.

4. You will not need to rely on referrals and word-of-mouth advertising only. Your Book will be your advertising agency.

5. You will not need to convince your clients of your credentials. Your Book will act as your portfolio.

It would not be an exaggeration to say that your Book works as your physical presence on the desk, bag, shelf, screen, etc., of your clients, prospects, and other audiences like your community and industry bodies.

The Book makes them think of you, reminds them of your Business, reiterates your skills, and drives them to contact you.

In one Master Stroke, you go from hunting for ways to expand your Business to being pursued by clients and flooded with opportunities.

Your Book can reach farther than you ever could!

Now that you're hooked on the incredible benefits of writing a book, it's time to surprise you even more…

In the next chapter, we will discuss how you can address the concerns and challenges specific to you as an Architect and further build your Business by writing a Book.

CHAPTER 3

IT'S YOUR STORY! NO ONE ELSE CAN TELL IT BETTER!

Architects are responsible for the beauty, functionality, safety, ergonomics, and ecological sustainability of all the buildings around us, including our homes and places of work. They create lovingly and with patience the world we inhabit. Yet, the synergy between an Architect and their client is often out of balance. The relationship often tends to be lopsided.

This lopsided relationship can result in the loss of big money and causes high levels of stress both for the Architect and the client. Some researchers have pointed out that crores of Rupees can be flushed down the drain because of lack of communication and failure to plan together by the Architect and the client.

It would be wonderful if the Architect could explain to the client clearly and precisely the steps and processes that would help the project run smoothly and speedily toward satisfactory completion. The Great news is, with your Book, you can do just that.

With the help of your Book, you can allow the client into your world, the pressures, the challenges, and every little detail that sometimes derails an entire project because you and your client do not speak the same language.

Through your Book, you can create empathy for your challenges, and you can showcase your innovations. You can teach people how to make their buildings eco-friendly and sustainable.

As an Architect, through your Book, you can create awareness amongst your clients about monetizing their buildings by minimizing running costs with cutting-edge design innovation and the use of new-age materials.

By sharing this knowledge through your Book, establish yourself as an expert, attract more Business than before, and contribute to the greater well-being of society and humanity by creating awareness of crucial issues and their solutions.

Let us enumerate the top reasons that would specifically benefit Architects by writing a BOOK.

Top 10 Reasons why Architects must write a Book!

1. Your Book can help educate clients about realistic Design Expectations by sharing basic technical info with them.

2. Your Book can work as a guideline to clear communication between you and your client, helping to bridge the gap between Expectation-Delivery Mismatch.

3. Use your Book to educate your clients and prospects on the right way to choose an Architect who is the best fit for their needs.

4. Use your Book to sensitize your clients to the challenges you face while sticking to deadlines such as;

   – Clearances, registrations, licenses, red tape, and other governmental regulations

   – Constant changes in designs or directions by the clients

   – Delayed decision making or reverts by the client

   – Delay in progress payments

   – Beauracracy in the client's organization

   – Delayed deliveries by vendors despite constant follow-ups

   – Unexpected Labour unrest

   – Etc.

   If they could understand and empathize with all the reasons that can cause delivery deadlines to go haywire, they would find it easy to trust you.

5. Use your Book to create awareness about Green and Eco-Friendly initiatives amongst your audience, showing them the possibility of an Energy-Efficient and Sustainable World.

   Through your Book, you can showcase how everyone can Maximize Energy-Efficiency and Minimize the Impact of building on Human Health and the Environment with only a little conscious effort.

   This would go along way in battling climate change concerns and help conserve our dwindling natural resources. **This strategy helps humanity and the planet while positioning you as a Climate- Change Warrior.**

6. Through your Book, you can teach your clients, prospects and, society at large how to monetize their buildings. Their Buildings are perhaps the most significant investments people make. You, as an Architect, are the best person to guide them on how to make a building work for them instead of working to maintain the building.

7. Use your Book as an opportunity to conduct a dialog and get into a conversation with other agencies like Contractors and Project Management Consultants, Interior Designers, etc., who directly impact the quality of work. This act would help you and the entire community as you enumerate and address the major pain points and suggest ground rules and practical solutions for a smoother interface between agencies.

8. Through your Book, you can highlight your achievements and the achievements of your peers and predecessors, thus promoting and celebrating the entire industry. When the industry grows as a whole, you stand to grow too.

9. Use the experiences and insight gathered over the years to guide and mentor other Architects through your Book to function smoothly, thus making a remarkable contribution to the industry and people's lives.

10. The Most important reason is listed below:

You, an Architect, should write a book not only for technical and Business reasons but also because you have valuable Life-Lessons to impart. You, my friends, are perhaps the Best Life Coaches without even realizing it because:

- You know the value of laying a solid foundation. As with your buildings, so with life. Anything worthwhile can only be built on a strong foundation.

- You are masters of making the best use of available resources. This applies to human life too. Everyone needs to make the best use of their circumstances and resources instead of waiting for more.

- Sticking to disciplined delivery deadlines is second nature to you. Discipline and scheduling are crucial to succeeding in life too.

- Planning right down to the last detail is an integral part of your profession. Planning before action is the way to win in life too.

- While you know how to stick to deadlines, you retain the ability to be flexible and adaptable in the face of new challenges on-site every day. Life is no different; to survive and thrive, it is essential to e flexible and adaptable and to take challenges in your stride.

- Multi-tasking successfully and coordinating seamlessly with various agencies is a cake-walk to you; this quality is needed to be successful in life too.

These are just the top 10 reasons, the list of reasons and benefits of writing a Book are endless, and we could go on for ages and pages, but the top 10 reasons alone are enough proof to begin on that Book right now...

CHAPTER 4

LIMITATIONS ARE AN ILLUSION: IT'S TIME TO GET THAT SKY SCRAPER UP!

We completely understand what is going through your mind right now!

All the reasons to not write a Book are crowding your mind. As much as you want to overcome your above-listed challenges, your mind tells you that you can not write a book. Argue for your limitations, and sure enough, they are yours, well, not this time.

It's time to break the barriers!

Let's talk about the Elephant in the room. Let's list all the possible reasons that could be keeping you from writing your Book and cementing your position as an expert in your industry, leading to more Impact and income.

- "I am an Architect and not a writer."
- "I do not know how to write a book."
- "I am too young (or too old) to write a book."
- "I do not know anyone from the publishing industry."
- "No one knows me."
- "I am too busy to write a book."
- "I do not have the money to publish a book."

Believe us; the list is endless.

It's time to bust those myths that you may be having about writing a book.

Myth #1

A book cannot bring profit for my Business!

Reality Check: A book may or may not bring profit. If it is written well to roar in the market, there can be no reason why the Book will not bring in Business and why its Author will not be flooded with name and fame.

Forget the Book; the Book cover alone can create magic and have a massive public impact.

Gullybaba Publication has devised the IIC Protocol for the cover page design of all their books from years of experience.

The acronym IIC stands for Impact-Integrate-Compel. We design the cover pages of our books following this protocol so that they are geared up for creating the maximum reach and Impact.

Quoting here just one example out of the several where the Cover alone was enough to bring rewards and Recognition:

> **The CEO of Blue Consulting, Mr Chandan Goayal, Author of "How to Manufacture Time" used his Book to establish Authority, and that created magic. His Book was launched at the International Book Fair, 2020, Jan, in Pragati Maidan, New Delhi. He got immense recognition and appreciation through the launch, and he has been able to make a massive impact on prospects and clients, which are largely CFOs of 100Cr worth companies.**

Myth #2

A book will not bring Authority!

Reality Check: This is another big myth that most people subscribe to. Recall from your own experience whenever someone is introduced as an Author in addition to their other designation, it never fails to impress the audience, including you.

Now visualize the same scenario with your introduction prefixed with "Author." Yes!!! You got it. You will receive the same Respect and Recognition as an authority.

You will be greeted with open arms at meetings and thunderous applause at seminars etc.

When you send your Book along with a hypnotic cover letter, you will instantly be perceived as an Authority and welcomed eagerly. This technique has earned respect for all those authors who have adopted this.

It has enabled them to control their conversations with clients, assert their Authority, and have clients agree to their terms and charges readily.

> *Mr. Sanjay Kumar, Real Estate Demand Generation Expert, authored two books for a different set of clients and was perceived as an Authority in that field in no time. Due to this, he started his coaching business from 1-2-1 to 1 to Many and has grown his business multi-fold.*

Myth #3

But I am not an Expert!

Reality Check: Self-doubt is the biggest silent killer of success and dreams. A majority of people suffer from it. Think of any of the big names in their fields like Sachin Tendulkar in Cricket, Mr. Bachhan in Cinema, or Lata Mangeshkar Ji in Music, and many others were they born as experts or were they experts right when they started.

Yes, that's right. Writing a Book is the first step in your journey to becoming an expert and not the other way round.

Taking that first step can be challenging; we understand, that is why I have created and promoted the concept of an 'Insta-Book,' which is a Booklet. You can introduce your potential to people by beginning with an "Insta-Book" and then graduating to a full-fledged book confidently.

> *Vivek Pathak authored an Insta-Book on finance,"From Mediocre to Wealthy" he is a highly successful financial planner and consultant, and that Book established him as an expert. As a result, he was published in the HT, the Economic Times, and severalother prestigious newspapers.*

Myth #4

I am not a Writer; I need to be good at Writing!

Reality Check: Most people think language and writing skills are the essence of writing books, so they cite their linguistic inferiority as the main reason for not writing a book. However, a Book is about its message, its content, and its value. A Book is not simply about language; it is all about communication. Big words and fancy language are great, but they are not the actual value of a book.

We have come across several reasonably competent and knowledgeable people who don't permit themselves to write a book citing Linguistic Lack as an excuse. What a pity! What a missed opportunity!

As a writer, your only job is to visualize and conceptualize a book. The rest will be taken care of by the experts; people, who are adept at doing these things. Take the example of Film Making. Do you think the director does everything related to the film even though they are the captain of the ship?

Certainly not! The Director Visualizes, Conceptualizes, and oversees the process. They are ably supported by the actors, scriptwriters, cinematographers, sound experts, etc., and together they create a beautiful product.

Similarly, even if you consider yourself linguistically challenged, **you can create the first draft of your Book in less than 5 hours through Book Mind Mapping and hand it over to an expert content developer and then to the editor for editing.**

Once you follow the systems and templates and the science of getting a book ready in 7 days, writing a Book is truly easy! It is then time to watch your creation on the shelf & online platforms like Amazon/Flipkart within 7 days. See for yourself how it is being sold on these platforms, and voila; Now you are a Bestselling Author!

> *I can see the visible difference in Client Interactions and getting business from them since I started sending them my books. Since its launch, I have been converting 1 client every fortnight effortlessly. –Rohit Surendra Nagia, Founder-Metricchant Design Attributes Pvt. Ltd. Author of two books, "Money Generating Building 2.0" & "Creating Urbane Hq's: The 1st Step".*

Myth #5

Even 24 hours are not enough; How do I find the time to write!

Reality Check: This is one of the most common reasons cited by entrepreneurs and professionals as an excuse for not writing a book.

Mind you, Phil Knight, the creator of Nike, the shoe and/Sportswear brand, had the same time as you have. Nonetheless, he wrote the book Shoe Dog: A Memoir by Phil Knight.

Therefore, it's time to stop making excuses and start writing.

Importantly, book writing does not involve so much time.

The content you serve your readers doesn't have to be huge; it has to be of value. It is vital to establish your credibility, and for that you can easily start with an Insta-Book-Influencer, A proprietary tool designed by me for high success and revenue impact.

An **Insta-book-Influencer is a psychologically designed** book in the least number of words, completely and dedicatedly focused towards marketing your product or services, leading to build your authority, credibility and influence.

It is not 200, 300, or 500 pages long. It is about 30 pages of High-Impact Power Content rooted in psychological marketing and can be written even in a matter of hours.

> ***Mr. Vinod K Pandita, CEO of Perception Management Consulting Pvt. Ltd. managed to author his Book in just 16 hours following the templates and guidelines shared in this Book.***

By now, we are sure that you are all geared up to write your Book and are rearing to get started; we will make it even easier for you. In the next chapter, we will show you why Architects can transition into writers smoothly and seamlessly.

So let's move on; we know you are super excited, so are we...

CHAPTER 5

THE MAGIC IS ALWAYS WITHIN; THE WRITER ALREADY EXISTS IN YOU!

In the previous chapter, Ankur and I have already busted the myths that could have been limiting you from writing your Book. This chapter will show how you, as an Architect, you already have what it takes to be a writer.

"Architecture is a way of thinking about the world very similar in structure to writing a book," opined Rem Koolhaas, the world-famous Dutch Architect.

As a publisher, I can assure you that it is not difficult to transition from Architect to Author. Here are some of the intersections and interfaces that will show you that you already possess the perspective and skill set needed to craft a Book:

Think of the e-mails you draft and send out to your clients multiple times a day. Each e-mail is clear, concise and intended to explain and communicate things to the receiver.

If you were to compile your e-mails alone for a few months, my friend, you would have an exciting book ready and in your hands already.

Now think of all the WhatsApp messages you write and answer, literally throughout the day. Answering queries, clearing doubts, giving information, offering suggestions and guidance, you are basically a writer every day of your life. The only limitation is that you don't realise it.

Let's also remind you of all your conversations with your clients, vendors, and associates all day. Imagine if you could record and transcribe all those conversations into printed words. Believe me, you would have not just a book but a series of books in your hands all written by you and did I just hear you say that you are an architect, not a writer.

In every conversation, you explain and share things in clear well-formed language that communicates exactly what you want to say, and that is exactly what a book does.

The writer already exists within you, my friend!

Now that you know the magic is within and that you are already a writer. I am sure you are ready and excited to begin on your Book, and we will show you how to polish the craft of writing to actually create your Best Seller and establish yourself as a sought-after expert in the following few chapters.

CHAPTER 6

NOT JUST ANY BOOK; THIS IS A BEST SELLER!

By now, you are entirely aware of the benefits of writing a Book for your profile and your Business, and you are ready and excited to start on your Book.

The exceptional template and tips that we will share with you have been developed through extensive research and have brought Sure-Shot-Success to hundreds of First-Time Authors.

We are delighted to share this template with you as a Thank-You for taking action to shift your life and Business into a higher zone by choosing this Book.

So let's begin right away…

Writing an Insta Book will help you reach 60 % more people than an ordinary book as it has been proven that people have shorter attention spans these days.

An Insta Book is your most powerful tool to activate your business and your marketing.

In a scenario where 16000 books are launched every day you really have to stand out to make the desired Impact.

An Insta-book-Influencer is a psychologically designed book in the least number of words, completely and dedicatedly focused towards marketing your product or services, leading to build your authority, credibility and influence.

It evokes the appropriate emotions in your readers and clients and compels them to respond to you and choose you.

An Insta Book is written on the basis of the IIC protocol which means to impact, integrate, and compel.

An Insta Book is not about the pressure of sales, it's about positioning you as an Expert "Pain Resolver"

Once you are established as the go to expert in your field, people with the need and resources will definitely seek your product and services.

Identify the 'WHY' and Find a Purpose

Before you begin writing, it is crucial to answer the 'Why' of your Book; what is your aim of writing a Book, is it to further your Business? Is it to spread a message? Is it to offer a solution? Is it to reveal a research or innovation? Is it to build a community or to mentor others??? The Whys can be innumerable; it will be different for different people because we are all unique. Finding the why will take a bit of Soul-Searching; however, once you have found it, it is what will keep you going; it will not let you rest until you fulfill your purpose.

Being clear on the why will ignite in you a sense of purpose, and a sense of purpose is what fuels a project. A sense of purpose is necessary to keep the project on track and the passion pulsating to reach the finish line.

Begin With The End In Mind; Work Backwards

Reverse-Planning (RP) is the best approach to writing a Book. Before you begin writing and after you identify your why you must spend some time visualizing the End. Not the literal ending of the Book but the finishing of the project.

Think about the day you will launch the Book you have worked sincerely on to its audience. Visualize those feelings of joy and fulfillment. Visualize the sense of pride of a job well done and the incredibly amazing feeling of holding a 'Dream-Fulfilled' in your hand finally.

Right, when you are immersed in these feelings is the time to make a crucial decision. DECIDE ON THE LAUNCH DATE OF YOUR BOOK!!!

As an experienced publisher, the first thing I ask Authors when they are sure about writing a Book is,"What is the LAUNCH DATE of your Book?"

Deciding on a launch date right in the beginning will help you schedule all your tasks and stick to your deadlines. If you leave the Launch Date open-ended, you will always find more excuses to delay the project.

Trust Your Publishing Team

It is an arduous task to mark your presence in the Best Seller club. If the Book is not written strongly and clearly, you will end up with a Bubble Book tag,i.e.,a book that fails to impress the audience and will not give you the desired results.

However, Ankur and I have promised to show you how to craft not just any Book but a Book that has the maximum possibility of becoming a Best Seller.

My publishing house has an excellent record of success, and if there were just one piece of advice that we had to give you, it would be this:

Trust and follow instructions from your publishing team. When the publishing team and the Author work in unison, things are destined for greatness and success. Following their guidance and taking baby steps at the appropriate time is sure to leave you with a Best Seller in your name.

A. Laying The Groundwork

1. Write all the specific goals or desired outcomes that you have/wish for your Book.

    ____

    ____

    ____

    ____

    ____

2. What is your audience's central problem or concern that you can solve by writing this Book?

    ____

    ____

    ____

    ____

    ____

3. What is the conversation likely to be going on in your readers' heads, and how can you hook them using this conversation?

    ____

    ____

    ____

    ____

    ____

4. What do you get paid for your expertise?

____

____

____

____

____

5. What topic or subject are you most passionate and knowledgeable about?

____

____

____

____

____

6. What is your favourite hobby?

____

____

____

____

____

7. What kind of people (designation, age group, profession, etc.) come to you for advice?

____

____

____

____

____

With all the exclusive tips and techniques Ankur and I have shared with you till now, you are ready and equipped to write and market your Best Seller.

This Book will indeed prove to be the pivot-point of your life with a measurable change of Before and After.

In the following concluding chapter, we will show you how to move up the Hierarchy Of Desire to be at the top of your game and become a celebrity in your field.

Excited!!!! Then let's move on to the finish line…

CHAPTER 7

MASTER OF THE GAME; YOU, VERSION 2.0!

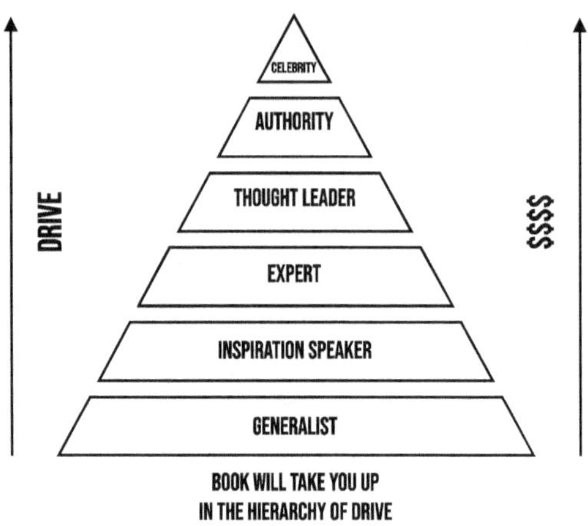

Yes!!!! That is YOU right there at the top of the pyramid!!!

Study the illustration of what I call the hierarchy of drive above very carefully. If you take action and follow the techniques and methodologies we have shared in this Book and my other books and work closely with us, there should be no reason why you would not scale this pyramid to become the "Master of the Game."

I'm probably not the first to present this idea, but I believe that there exists magic in a book for almost anyone looking to grow a business and explode their income and Impact.

The concept of the hierarchy is that as your saleability increases in the eyes of your ideal client, so does your attractiveness and your charges.

As we have already discussed in detail in the previous chapters, the real magic is how your Book propels you from a generalist or even a specialist to expert, and eventually to a Leader/Authority and if you adopt the MM Methodology to Celebrity status even.

As I often say at Pendown Press, "As you scale up in the hierarchy, you shift from hunting for clients to becoming hunted by clients."

Having empowered you with all the tools to craft and market your Book, Ankur and I are super excited to see you write and publish your first Book.

- ✓ Imagine the number of people your Book will inspire.
- ✓ Imagine the solutions that you'll provide through your Book.
- ✓ Imagine sharing your story and lifting people through your words.
- ✓ Imagine making a difference in someone else's life. Isn't that what life is all about?

Write your Book for the right reasons because it is your intent that will shape the Book and its success. Write your Book from the perspective of someone who passionately wants to add value to people's lives. Write your Book with pure intentions.

As you give, you get so much more in return. This is the simple formula to succeed! Give, and you will receive!

CHAPTER 8

WHEN TO START?

In this Book, we have presented all the benefits that a Book can bring to your business and your personal brand.

Not only that, but we have also shared with you the tools and techniques to begin right away.

In today's times, if you are not using an Insta-Book-Influencer to create an impact, believe me, you are throwing huge business, market share, clients and profits down the drain, or you are gifting them to a competitor who is more proactive than you.

At the beginning of the Book, I have given you examples of many business owners and consultants who have used the Insta-Book-Influencer format to create massive Impact and generate revenue like never before. And those were only a fraction of the long list of successful Insta-Book-Influencers I have helped till now.

If you are determined to reach the top of the pyramid and impact more lives while multiplying your income using the

First Tool of the MM Methodology (Marketing Magnetism Methodology). In that case, all you need to do is give me 15 minutes of your precious time. Reach out to me:

BestsellerWithDinesh.com

For My FREE-Live Webinars
www.BestsellerWithDinesh.com/live

I am eager to support you, my Architect friends, for
I believe that we can together build a better world, one Book at a time.
Sincerely wishing you a Best Seller!

Dinesh Verma